S

Dominie Press, Inc.

When the sun shines on things, it makes shadows.

When the sun shines on a tree, it makes a tree shadow.

When the sun shines on me,
it makes my shadow.

When the sun is high,
my shadow is short.

When the sun is low,
my shadow is long.

The sun shines on the Earth and makes an Earth shadow on the moon.

The Earth shadow gets bigger...

... and **bigger**...

... and **bigger**.

The Earth shadow covers the moon.

Then the Earth shadow
gets smaller...

... and smaller...

... **and** smaller.

A full moon
has no Earth shadow.